Skills & Practice

for OCR

Steven Croft

UNIVERSITY PRESS

Oxford University Press is a department of the University of Oxford. It furthers the University's objective of excellence in research, scholarship, and education by publishing worldwide in

Oxford   New York

Auckland   Cape Town   Dar es Salaam   Hong Kong   Karachi
Kuala Lumpur   Madrid   Melbourne   Mexico City   Nairobi
New Delhi   Shanghai   Taipei   Toronto

With offices in

Argentina   Austria   Brazil   Chile   Czech Republic   France   Greece
Guatemala   Hungary   Italy   Japan   South Korea   Poland   Portugal   Singapore
Switzerland   Thailand   Turkey   Ukraine   Vietnam

Oxford is a registered trade mark of Oxford University Press in the UK and in certain other countries

© Oxford University Press 2011

The moral rights of the author have been asserted.

Database right Oxford University Press (maker)

First published 2011

All rights reserved. No part of this publication may be reproduced, stored in a retrieval system, or transmitted in any form or by any means, without the prior permission in writing of Oxford University Press, or as expressly permitted by law, or under terms agreed with the appropriate reprographics rights organization. Enquiries concerning reproduction outside the scope of the above should be sent to the Rights Department, Oxford University Press, at the address above.

You must not circulate this book in any other binding or cover and you must impose this same condition on any acquirer

Third party website addresses referred to in this publication are provided by Oxford University Press in good faith and for information only and Oxford University Press disclaims any responsibility for the material contained therein.

British Library Cataloguing in Publication Data
Data available

ISBN: 978-0-19-913886-9

10 9 8 7 6 5 4 3 2 1

Printed in Great Britain by Ashford Colour Press Ltd., Gosport.

Acknowledgements

Illustrations and layout by Q2A.

Contents

Preparing for Assessment — 4
Preparing for Controlled Assessment — 4
Preparing for the written exam — 8
Key skills — 11

Unit 1 Extended Literary Text and Imaginative Writing — 15
Controlled Assessment insight — 15
Section A: Extended literary text — 18
Section B: Imaginative writing — 25
Boost your grade — 29

Unit 2 Speaking, Listening and Spoken Language — 30
Section A: Speaking and Listening — 33
Section B: Spoken language — 39
Boost your grade — 44

Unit 3 Information and Ideas — 46
Exam insight — 46
Section A: Reading non-fiction and media texts — 48
Section B: Writing information and ideas — 51
Boost your grade — 59

Glossary — 61

Preparing for Assessment

To do well in your English Language GCSE it is important that you understand what each element of your course involves so that you can prepare for it effectively. Your assessment will consist of three units:

Unit 1 (A651): Extended Literary Text and Imaginative Writing (Controlled Assessment)
Unit 2 (A652): Speaking, Listening and Spoken Language (Controlled Assessment)
Unit 3 (A653): Information and Ideas (2 hour written exam)

Preparing for Controlled Assessment
What is Controlled Assessment?

Controlled Assessment is a way of assessing your work in a controlled situation. In Controlled Assessment units, the work that you produce for assessment will be completed in a supervised environment (possibly your classroom). It will be marked by your teacher and then moderated by your exam board. Unlike on examination, Controlled Assessment tasks are not unseen.

For GCSE English Language, Units 1 and 2 are both assessed by Controlled Assessment, partly through written tasks and partly through speaking and listening tasks. Altogether Controlled Assessment will make up 60% of your total marks.

The stages of Controlled Assessment

Controlled Assessment takes place in three stages:

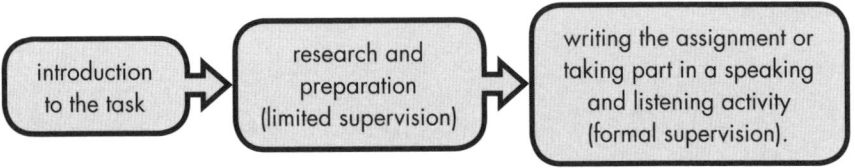

Preparing for Assessment

Introduction to the task
Your teacher will introduce you to the task and make sure that you know exactly what to do and what is required of you.

Research and preparation
During this part of the process you will be able to work under 'limited supervision' which means that you will be able to work without being directly supervised. You may also be able to work with other students and some of your work might be done outside the classroom.

Completing your assignment
This is where you write your final piece of work or take part in a speaking and listening activity that will be assessed as part of your final GCSE mark. You may be asked to write your written assignment in one session or your writing time may be split across more than one session. This stage will be completed under 'formal supervision' which means you will be supervised at all times and will not be allowed to use dictionaries, thesauruses, or spell checkers, or discuss your work with your teacher.

Preparing for your written assessment

The following points may be useful when preparing for your written assessment.

1. Planning
Once your teacher has introduced the task you will spend some time in lessons researching and preparing the topic of your assessment. During this time your teacher will be able to discuss the task with you but can only give you general advice.

At this stage make sure that:
- you plan how you are going to approach the task
- you organize and structure your ideas
- you use your research to inform and develop your own ideas
- you keep an accurate record of all the research materials you have used and where you found them.

Preparing for Assessment

2. Writing your response

You will write your assessment under formal supervision – this may take place as one long session or more than one shorter sessions. Remember to:
- do everything the task asks you to do
- write in Standard English using proper sentences and well-formed paragraphs – do not write in note form
- keep track of the time available and leave yourself enough time at the end for reading through and checking your work
- acknowledge all sources and quotations that you use.

3. Checking your work

When checking your work, make sure that:
- you have not made any spelling or punctuation errors
- you have used sentences and paragraphs correctly
- you have not made any grammatical mistakes
- you have done everything that the task asked.

4. Boost your grade

To achieve a top grade you must be able to:
- show through the relevance of your answer that you have a sophisticated understanding of the demands of the task
- structure your answer to ensure clarity and to produce deliberate effects to engage the reader and enhance with accurate spelling and punctuation
- use effective, imaginative and precise vocabulary with accurate spelling and punctuation
- use quotations and comparisons precisely to enhance your response

Preparing for your speaking and listening assessment

For GCSE English Language the speaking and listening assessment makes up 20% of your total mark. (A further 10% relates to the study of spoken language which is assessed through a written assignment.)

Preparing for Assessment

The skills you need to demonstrate are:
- presenting and listening to information and ideas
- responding appropriately to the questions and views of others
- making a range of effective contributions
- reflecting and commenting critically on your own and others' use of language
- participating in a range of real-life contexts in and outside the classroom
- adapting your speech to suit audience, purpose and context
- selecting and using a range of dramatic techniques and creative approaches to explore ideas, issues and texts in scripted and improvised role-play situations.

The following points may be useful when preparing for your speaking and listening assessments.

1. The assessment tasks

You will be assessed on three different activities:
- an individual extended contribution.
- a group activity
- a drama-focused activity.

The time allowed for the activities will depend on the nature of the tasks that are set.

2. Top tips for speaking

- Be enthusiastic about the topic of your task.
- Keep to the topic! Try to stay focused on what is being discussed.
- Do not repeat points that have already been made unless you have something new to add.
- Vary the tone of your voice.
- Do not interrupt other speakers; always be polite and sensitive to others.
- When you talk to an audience, make sure that your body language is positive; don't lean or slouch.
- Don't stare at the floor or look out of the window; focus on your audience and establish eye contact with them.
- Don't mumble – speak clearly and loud enough to be heard but without shouting.

Preparing for Assessment

3. Top tips for listening

- Always be involved in discussions even if you are just listening carefully to what is being said.
- When listening to a speaker, think about your body language. Face the speaker and offer your full attention. Make eye contact and give positive signals such as nodding and smiling.
- Don't look bored or uninterested; don't yawn or sigh.
- If you notice a speaker is nervous, try to put them at their ease. Give encouraging and positive signals and help out where necessary.

4. Boost your grade

To achieve a top grade you must be able to:
- highlight the most important details when talking about complex topics
- use a range of Standard English vocabulary and grammar confidently in appropriate contexts
- listen carefully and show that you understand what has been said by asking relevant and thoughtful questions
- shape the direction of a discussion and respond with flexibility to develop ideas and challenge assumptions
- encourage participation from other students and try to resolve any differences of opinion to achieve a positive outcome
- use appropriate dramatic approaches to create complex charactors in role-play
- explore and respond to complex issues in both formal and informal scenarios.

Preparing for the written exam

The written exam makes up 40% of your total marks for GCSE.

1. Planning and preparing

Careful planning and preparation is essential for success in your exam. You will undertake some of this preparation as part of your ongoing course and carry out some of it in the weeks immediately before you take the exam.

Preparing for Assessment

The following points may be useful when preparing for your written exam.

Throughout the course
- Become an active reader in everyday life. Read texts of all kinds. This will help you become familiar with the ways in which language is used to suit all kinds of audiences and purposes.
- Wide reading will also help you to improve your own vocabulary, sentence structures and understanding of how texts of different kinds are written and organized.
- When you read different kinds of texts, think about how writers use language to create particular effects.

Planning your revision
- Begin your revision in good time.
- Make sure that you know exactly what to expect on your exam paper and what it will require you to do. Ask your teacher for past papers and look at the sample questions in this book (as well as in your Student Book). Practise answering these questions in the same amount of time that you will have available in each exam.
- Look at the mark scheme for your exam paper – this will show you what the examiners are looking for. (Ask your teacher about this or find it on your exam board's website.)
- Identify areas you need to focus on and plan your revision time effectively – consider drawing up a timetable, fitting in all the topics and activities you intend to cover.
- Make sure that you are able to write accurately and fluently. If you have problems with any areas (e.g. spelling or punctuation), work on them to improve your skills before you sit the exam.

Preparing for Assessment

2. The question paper

You can save yourself a lot of time by being aware of what to expect on the question paper. You can find details about each assessment and question paper in the **insight** section at the start of each unit in this book.

This tells you the name of the unit you are covering and the level. Make sure you have the correct paper before you begin.

This lists any other materials you will receive alongside your exam booklet.

Read these instructions very carefully **before** you begin answering the questions and follow them exactly.

You should also read this additional information carefully before you begin.

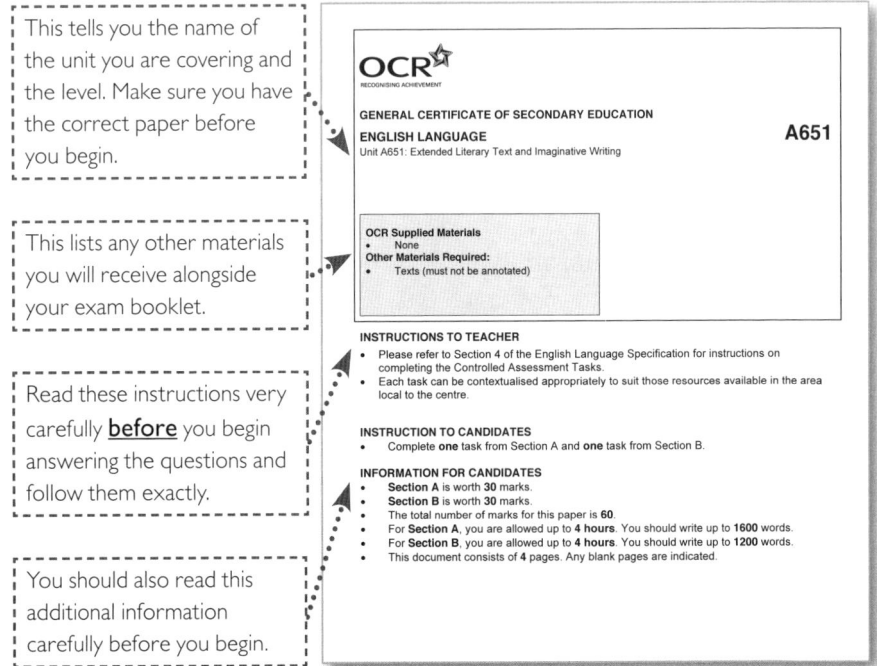

3. Planning and checking your answers

- Make sure that you read the questions carefully before you start to write anything.
- Set aside a few minutes to think about and plan your answers. Some forward planning is essential if you are to produce the best answers you can.
- Use notes to plan your answers – don't waste valuable time writing in full sentences.
- Make sure that you leave yourself a few minutes at the end of the exam to check your spelling, punctuation, grammar and paragraphing.

PREPARING FOR ASSESSMENT

Preparing for Assessment

4. Boost your grade

To achieve a top grade you must be able to:
- write confidently and skilfully, using style and structural features to engage readers
- use a wide range of vocabulary and sentence structures accurately and imaginatively
- ensure your writing is entirely appropriate to audience and purpose

Key skills

Technical errors in your writing can cost you precious marks. They wil not be assessed in unit 1 section A, but they will be assessed as part of unit 1 section B (imaginative writing) and unit 3 section B (writing information and ideas). During your course you need to do all you can to improve the standard of your written English. You can do this by:
- taking note of your teacher's corrections
- making yourself aware of particular words you spell incorrectly or any punctuation marks you have problems with
- working on the areas you know cause you problems
- checking your work through carefully.

Spelling

Correct spelling will help you to get higher marks at GCSE. The following suggestions will help you to improve your spelling.
- Read as much as possible – seeing words in print can help you visualize them as you write.
- Identify the words that you frequently spell incorrectly and work at learning these words.
- Always read through your written work and check it for mistakes.

Preparing for Assessment

Look at these commonly misspelt words. Can you identify what is wrong with each one? Write down the correct spelling of each word.

beautiful	decieve	restaurent
begining	knowlege	rythm
buisness	neccesary	sincerly
concious	recieve	untill

Create your own list of words that you sometimes spell incorrectly and watch out for them in your writing.

Commonly confused words

Some spelling mistakes happen because one word is confused with a similar word. The list below gives examples:

you're – your
- **You're** going to be in trouble if you do that.
- I like **your** new bike.

being – been
- You are **being** very annoying.
- I have **been** such a fool!

know – now – no
- I **know** you can do this.
- It is time to leave **now**.
- We have **no** homework today.

where – wear – were
- **Where** did I put my bag?
- I don't know what I am going to **wear** for the party.
- They **were** really looking forward to the holidays.

loose – lose
- That knot is coming **loose**.
- Don't **lose** the money I gave you.

PREPARING FOR ASSESSMENT

Preparing for Assessment

Punctuation

Like spelling, correct punctuation is important if you are to achieve the grade you are capable of. Be aware of any particular kind of punctuation that you have problems with and work on improving it.

Here are some key punctuation marks you should be able to use accurately in your writing:
- full stops
- question marks
- speech marks
- apostrophes.

Full stops

As you know, sentences end with a full stop. However, how you divide your writing up into sentences depends on what you are writing about and the effects you want to achieve. Make sure, though, that you always write in complete sentences that make sense as stand-alone units. Another common mistake is to string together completed statements with commas instead of using full stops to separate them.

Question marks

You will probably be quite clear about when to use question marks. The main problem students have is remembering to put them in – particularly when writing under pressure.

Remember:
- do not put a full stop and a question mark together
- do not use a question mark with an indirect question.

> Look at these two sentences. One of them is an example of a direct question and the other an indirect question.
>
> 1. *Have you finished your revision programme*
> 2. *She asked me if I had finished my revision programme*
>
> Which sentence do you think needs a question mark?

Preparing for Assessment

Speech marks
The list below sets out some key things to remember.
- Only put the speech marks around the words actually spoken.
- Punctuation marks relating to the words spoken, such as question marks, go inside the speech marks.
- Remember to start a new line each time a different person speaks.

Apostrophes
Apostrophes are used for two main purposes:
1. To show where letters have been missed out in shortening words or running two words together (these are called 'contractions'), e.g. *you are – you're; we had – we'd*.
2. They can be used to show that something belongs to someone or something (these are possessive apostrophes), e.g. *Mark's car*. Watch out especially for <u>its</u> and <u>it's</u>. 'It's' is a contraction of 'it is', whereas 'its' indicates something belonging to 'it', e.g. *The dog ate its food*.

Grammar

Grammatical errors can make your work harder to read. This often means that your meaning is less clear to the examiner. If possible, read your work aloud – if it sounds wrong then it probably is. Some common mistakes are set out below.

Changing tense
Sometimes tenses are incorrectly switched within a paragraph, sometimes even within a sentence. For example:

Sue ran as fast as she could but missed her bus. She sits down and starts to cry.

'Sue ran as fast as she could but missed her bus.' This is written in the past tense. The next sentence, however is written in the present tense: 'She sits down and starts to cry.' These tenses should agree. The correct version would read:
Sue ran as fast as she could but missed her bus. She <u>sat</u> down and <u>started</u> to cry.

Could of, would of, should of
Another common mistake is muddling 'of' with 'have' because of the similarity in the way these words sound. The correct way of writing these phrases is: *could <u>have</u>, would <u>have</u>, should <u>have</u>*. For example: *Sue should <u>have</u> met Danny at six and she would <u>have</u> been early if she could <u>have</u> caught the bus.*

PREPARING FOR ASSESSMENT

Unit 1
Extended Literary Text and Imaginative Writing

Controlled Assessment insight

Unit summary

This unit is worth 30% of the overall GCSE English Language mark. It is divided into two sections.

Unit 1: Extended Literary Text and Imaginative Writing

Section A: Extended literary text (15%)

Section B: Imaginative writing (15%)

Section A: Extended literary text

For this part of the unit you need to produce **one** piece of writing in response to your reading of a literary text. The text can be chosen from those on the OCR list or one set by your teacher. It can be prose, drama, poetry or literary non-fiction.

You will have up to **four hours** to produce your final piece of work under controlled conditions. The recommended maximum word length for your final piece is up to **1600 words**. Candidates who exceed the stated word length will not be unduly penalised when their work is relevant to the task.

Section B: Imaginative writing

For this part of the unit you need to complete **one** exercise made up of **two** linked tasks. For the tasks you can choose **either** Personal and Imaginative Writing **or** Prose Fiction.

Each exercise will contain a core task and a choice of three linked tasks. You will have up to **four hours** to produce your final piece of work under controlled conditions. The recommended word length for your final piece is up to **1200 words**.

Extended Literary Text and Imaginative Writing

Assessment Objectives

This unit tests Assessment Objectives 3 and 4. Here is a breakdown of the skills tested.

Section A
AO3 Studying written language

> **AO3**
>
> Read and understand texts, selecting material appropriate to purpose, collating from different sources and making comparisons and cross-references as appropriate.

This means that you will need to understand the text you read and choose appropriate material from it to answer questions. It also means that you will need to make comparisons and cross-references within your chosen text.

> **AO3**
>
> Develop and sustain interpretations of writers' ideas and perspectives.

This means that you will need to interpret ideas expressed by writers and show that you understand their views. You will need to comment on inferences and discuss how writers make their meaning clear.

> **AO3**
>
> Explain and evaluate how writers use linguistic, grammatical, structural and presentational features to achieve effects and engage and influence the reader.

This means you need to explain clearly how writers use language and presentational features to create effects and influence the reader.

Extended Literary Text and Imaginative Writing

Section B

AO4 Writing

AO4

Write to communicate clearly, effectively and imaginatively, using and adapting forms and selecting vocabulary appropriate to task and purpose in ways which engage the reader.

This means that you should write effectively using language to suit the particular audience and purpose of the task you have been given.

AO4

Organize information and ideas into structured and sequenced sentences, paragraphs and whole texts, using a variety of linguistic and structural features to support cohesion and overall coherence.

This means that you should organize your ideas into sentences and paragraphs that link together to create an effective piece of writing.

AO4

Use a range of sentence structures for clarity, purpose and effect, with accurate punctuation and spelling.

This means that you should use different kinds of sentences to suit the purpose of your writing. You should also ensure that your spelling and punctuation is accurate.

Extended Literary Text and Imaginative Writing

Section A: Extended literary text

Whether the extended literary text you are studying is a drama, prose or poetry, you will still need to examine how the writer uses language to create precise effects. Drama is different from prose in that it is written to be seen in performance rather than being read. When studying drama you should therefore think about how the text might work on stage.

Drama and literary prose texts

Drama and prose texts have common features. They both have:
- characters at the centre of the action
- themes or key ideas
- a setting or settings within which the action takes place.

Characters

When looking at characters, whether in novels, short stories or plays, you should always remember that they are not real people but the **creations** of the writers. If they seem real and convincing it is because the skill of the writer makes them so.

Writers can create realistic characters in various ways:
- **description** – writers can describe their characters, e.g. what they look like and how they dress
- **actions** – writers can depict what the characters do, how they behave, respond to situations, etc.
- **dialogue** – writers can reveal a lot about a character by what he or she says (this is vital in a play); what other characters say about them is important too
- **thoughts and feelings** – in a novel the narrator may describe how characters feel; in a play, soliloquies are often used to reveal this.

Choose a few passages or sections from the novel or play that you are studying that reveal something about one of the key characters.
- Make notes on how the writers use language to present the character(s).
- Make a list of key quotations with notes explaining the significance of each one.

Extended Literary Text and Imaginative Writing

Themes and ideas
Most novels and plays are concerned with certain key ideas and themes. Themes can be about almost anything and a novel or play might explore more than one.

> Think about the text you are studying and make a list of the key ideas and themes that it contains.

Writers explore their themes and ideas in various ways, for example through:
- the development of the storyline
- key speeches or dialogue
- the use of imagery or symbolism
- the use of setting and stage directions
- the actions of the characters.

> Using the text that you are studying, make a list of quotations that illustrate or refer to its key ideas or themes.

Setting
The setting of a novel or play is important because it creates the background against which the action takes place.
- In a novel, the writer will often use descriptive passages to create a sense of setting; in a play, look at the information given in stage directions.
- The setting can also be important in a symbolic way and may be linked to key ideas or themes.
- The setting in both novels and plays is often closely linked to atmosphere.

> Look at the settings created in the novel or play you are studying. Make notes on:
> - how the settings affect the development of the narrative or drama
> - the ways in which the writer creates a sense of a particular setting
> - the atmosphere created.

Extended Literary Text and Imaginative Writing

Literary non-fiction

Literary non-fiction covers a variety of kinds of writing, such as autobiography, travel writing, literary journalism, memoirs and biography. One thing they have in common is a central narrative that is factually accurate and written in a literary style.

To achieve this, the writer can use a variety of techniques. These are similar to those used in fictional literary texts, such as novels, and include:
- imagery – to present detailed description, perhaps using metaphors or similes to present a scene or situation or to describe feelings or emotions
- direct speech – to give a sense of immediacy and realism
- particular sentence structures – to create effects such as suspense or excitement.

When you are studying a literary non-fiction text, you should therefore approach it in just the same way as you would a fictional literary text – but remember that the characters are real and the narrative based on actual events.

> Re-read your literary non-fiction text and make notes on the techniques that the writer uses to create effects and present key ideas.

Poetry

Ideas and themes, and the way your chosen poet presents them, will be central to your reading of poems at GCSE. One or more of the themes shown on the next page will be relevant to the poems you are studying.

Extended Literary Text and Imaginative Writing

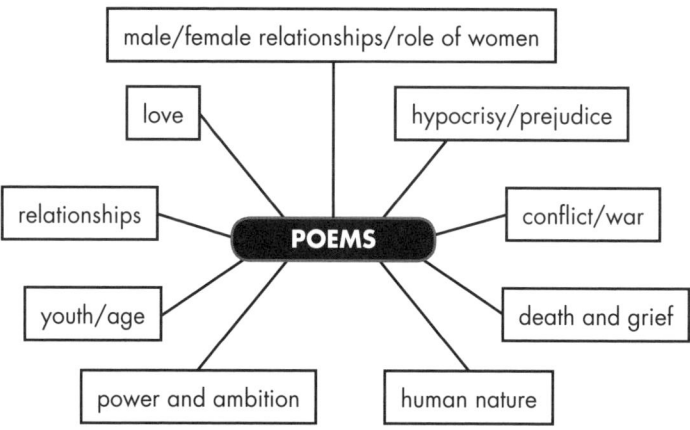

In the Controlled Assessment you will complete a task in which you are asked to explain how a particular theme is important in the poems you are studying. One way of tackling this is to approach the poems in the following way.

1. Look carefully at the task and think about the theme and key ideas it involves.
2. Look at the range of poems you have studied and select those that best illustrate how your theme is explored and presented by the poet. (How many poems you select depends to some extent on the length and content of each. Consult your teacher about this.)
3. Re-read each poem to check your choices are the best ones possible. Revise your selection it necessary.
4. Re-read your chosen poems several times and make a brief note on each about how it is relevant to the theme you are exploring.
5. Look at each poem in more detail in relation to your question title.

Extended Literary Text and Imaginative Writing

Key questions and features
When reading your poems, think about:
- **What** the poems are about (their content)
- **How** the poet uses language in them (his/her techniques and style)
- **Why** the poet uses language in the way he or she does (what **effects** does he/she want to achieve?)

Read them again and pay attention to:
- the vocabulary the poet uses – which words has he/she chosen to use? Do you find any words or phrases particularly striking? What effect do they create?
- any imagery the poet uses such as:
  - metaphors
  - similes
  - personification
  - aural imagery, e.g. alliteration, onomatopoeia, assonance
- any use of rhyme
- the rhythm of the poem.

Read your selected poems and for each one make notes under the headings below.
- What the poem is about
- How the poet uses language in this poem
- The effect achieved by the use of language

In your notes refer to any features, such as striking vocabulary, imagery, rhyme and rhythm, and the <u>effects</u> these create.

Finish off by noting how these features contribute to the poet's exploration of the theme you are focusing on.

Extended Literary Text and Imaginative Writing

Preparing your notes for the extended literary text

Before you write your final piece your teacher will spend **between 60 and 90 minutes** introducing the task to you. You are then allowed about **25 hours** of preparation and research time. During this time you can prepare notes to use when writing under controlled conditions. When writing your final piece you are also allowed to have with you a clean copy of the text (i.e. no notes or annotations on it).

Your notes must:
- not contain a draft of your assignment and must be completely in note form
- be prepared entirely by you without help from anyone else.

Your teacher will check your notes to make sure they are suitable before your Controlled Assessment sessions begin.

What your notes can contain

Your notes can include any information you find helpful when writing your assignment, such as:
- the exact title of your task
- page references for particular parts of the text you want to refer to
- key quotations
- the names of characters you will focus on
- general notes on approaches or points to jog your memory
- the spelling of particular words.

On the next page is an example of the kinds of notes that you might make in preparation for the task: 'How does William Shakespeare present love and its effects in *Romeo and Juliet*?'

Extended Literary Text and Imaginative Writing

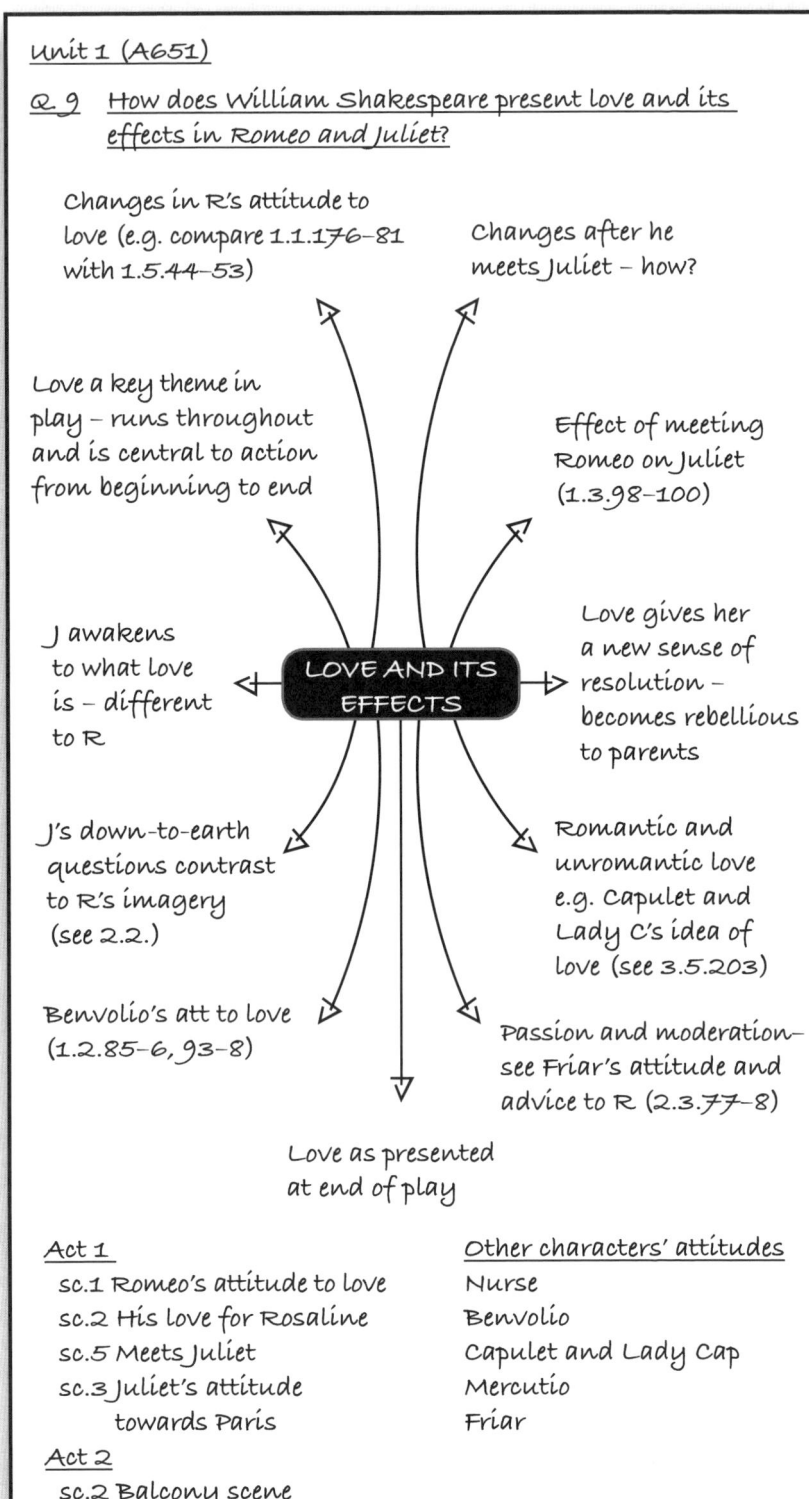

Unit 1 (A651)

Q.9 How does William Shakespeare present love and its effects in Romeo and Juliet?

- Changes in R's attitude to love (e.g. compare 1.1.176–81 with 1.5.44–53)
- Changes after he meets Juliet – how?
- Love a key theme in play – runs throughout and is central to action from beginning to end
- Effect of meeting Romeo on Juliet (1.3.98–100)
- J awakens to what love is – different to R
- **LOVE AND ITS EFFECTS**
- Love gives her a new sense of resolution – becomes rebellious to parents
- J's down-to-earth questions contrast to R's imagery (see 2.2.)
- Romantic and unromantic love e.g. Capulet and Lady C's idea of love (see 3.5.203)
- Benvolio's att to love (1.2.85–6, 93–8)
- Passion and moderation – see Friar's attitude and advice to R (2.3.77–8)
- Love as presented at end of play

Act 1
 sc.1 Romeo's attitude to love
 sc.2 His love for Rosaline
 sc.5 Meets Juliet
 sc.3 Juliet's attitude towards Paris
Act 2
 sc.2 Balcony scene

Other characters' attitudes
 Nurse
 Benvolio
 Capulet and Lady Cap
 Mercutio
 Friar

Extended Literary Text and Imaginative Writing

Section B: Imaginative writing

The second Controlled Assessment that you need to complete as part of Unit 1 is a piece of imaginative writing. For this you can choose to do **either** a piece of personal and imaginative writing **or** a piece of prose fiction.

Personal and imaginative writing

This is an example of the choice of tasks you will have.

---

1 PERSONAL AND IMAGINATIVE WRITING

   (a)   Write about a memorable holiday that you have had.

AND

Either

   b(i)   Write a leaflet to give people information about an interesting place to visit.

Or

   b(ii)   Write a review for a local newspaper on a particular holiday resort.

Or

   b(iii)   Write the text of a talk to persuade a group of young people to visit a particular historical, educational or recreational location. Use your own experiences as an example.

In this sort of writing, your key aim is to create a vivid picture of your particular subject or experience.

The easiest way of doing this is often to draw on your own ideas and experiences. Because of this, personal writing tends to be focused on you, so is usually written in the first person.

Remember – don't just stick to visual details when writing a description. Think about textures, tastes, smells and sounds too. This applies to **all** types of imaginative writing.

Extended Literary Text and Imaginative Writing

Prose fiction

This is an example of the choice of tasks you will have.

---

2 PROSE FICTION

  (a) Write a story entitled 'Deception'.

AND

Either

  b(i) Write a preview for a magazine giving information about the characters and setting of the story.

Or

  b(ii) Write the script of an internet interview with one or two key characters from your story in which the interviewer questions them about their behaviour in the story.

Or

  b(iii) Write a review of the story for a local reading group newsletter.

Thinking in advance about what your storyline will be is a good starting point when preparing for this assignment. To be successful, your story must hold the reader's interest from beginning to end.

When planning your storyline you need to think about:
- narrative viewpoint – first or third person
- who the key characters are
- the setting
- the atmosphere
- how the story will develop.

Extended Literary Text and Imaginative Writing

Making your writing more vivid

There are various techniques you can use in your imaginative writing to make it more vivid. Here are some of them:
- the use of imagery, e.g. similes and metaphors
- phonological devices, e.g. alliteration, onomatopoeia and assonance to create 'sound effects' in your writing
- different sentence types and structures to help to create a particular tone or mood – varying the length of sentences can change the rhythm or the pace of your writing
- the careful choice of adjectives and adverbs to describe smells, tastes, textures and sounds as well as sights.

However, you should avoid making your writing overly elaborate.

> Look at the examples of student writing below. One is filled with detail and one is more restrained in language use. Which do you think is most effective? Give your reasons.

> The wind tore through the trees like a wild, vicious animal that was on the rampage. Its howling, screaming, screeching voice felt like it was about to shatter the brittle, fragile glass-like windows. The banshee-like wailing went on and on and the monstrous, furious tumultuous waves smashed endlessly and mercilessly on the bleak, desolate, barren shore.

> The wind had risen and now was approaching gale force as it howled through phone wires and rattled the windows of the house like a lost soul trying to get in. The larger trees bent almost beyond their limits while smaller ones were torn from the soil and instantly disappeared into the darkness – carried away on the wind. In the background the roaring of the sea added to the tumult as mountainous waves swept up the deserted beach.

Extended Literary Text and Imaginative Writing

Planning your response

Here are some points to remember when planning your imaginative writing piece.

The opening
Your opening needs to make an impact – it should be lively and interesting and capture the reader's interest.

Developing your ideas
You need to keep the reader engaged in your writing.

In personal experience writing, you can achieve this by:
- creating a sense of personal voice – you could use the first person narrative style and include personal anecdotes
- using dialogue to add interest and immediacy
- making your description vivid.

In a story, you can achieve this by:
- pacing the action effectively
- creating interesting and convincing characters
- using dialogue to bring the story to life
- providing vivid description to create a sense of atmosphere and setting.

The ending
The ending should also make an impact on your reader. To do this effectively you could try:
- a 'shock' ending that takes the reader by surprise
- a 'twist in the tale' ending
- an ending that cleverly resolves all lose ends
- an open ending that leaves some questions unresolved and keeps the reader guessing
- an ending where everything finally becomes clear to the main character.

Preparing your notes for the imaginative writing assessment

You will be allowed about **15 hours** preparation and research time to think about your ideas and prepare your notes. They must be entirely your own work and not resemble a draft response.

Extended Literary Text and Imaginative Writing

Boost your grade

Studying written language: extended literary text

To achieve the best grade for your assessment you must:
- produce a clear and relevant response
- comments on a range of interpretations of the text as appropriate
- use carefully chosen references from the text to support and illustrate your points precisely
- comment on the writer's perspective in detail in your answer.

Imaginative writing

To achieve the best grade for your assessment, you must:
- produce a piece of lively, original writing that is aimed effectively at the correct audience and purpose
- structure your work and use paragraphs effectively to
- use a wide range of well-chosen engage the reader and imaginative vocabulary
- spell and punctuate your work accurately.

Unit 2
Speaking, Listening and Spoken Language

Controlled Assessment insight

Unit summary

This unit is worth 30% of the overall GCSE English Language mark. It is divided into two sections.

Unit 2: Speaking, Listening and Spoken Language

Section A: Speaking and Listening (20%)

Section B: Spoken Language (10%)

Section A: Speaking and listening

For this part of the unit you will complete **three** speaking and listening tasks. These tasks will require you to work both individually and within a group, exploring ideas, texts and issues in scripted and improvised work.

Section B: Spoken Language

For this part of the unit you will complete **one** written assessment on **either** the study of the spoken language of a public figure **or** language, media and technology or language and society.

Part A: The study of the Spoken Language of a Public Figure

For this option you will study the spoken language of a particular person in a specific context.

Part B: Language, Media and Technology or Language and Society

For this option you will consider how speech and the way people interact vary within different social situations and in different contexts. You will look at the influence of factors such as changing technologies, social groups and the passage of time. You will then use what you have learned to think about your own spoken language.

Speaking, Listening and Spoken Language

Assessment Objectives

This unit tests Assessment Objectives 1 and 2. Here is a breakdown of the skills tested.

Section A
AO1 Speaking and Listening

> **AO1**
>
> Speak to communicate clearly and purposefully; structure and sustain talk, adapting it to different situations and audiences; use Standard English and a variety of techniques as appropriate.

This means that you must be able to speak in different situations and adapt your speech to suit your audience and purpose. Your speech must be clear and effective.

> **AO1**
>
> Listen and respond to speakers' ideas, perspectives and how they construct and express their meanings.

This means that you need to listen carefully to what others say, be aware of how they say it and respond to them appropriately.

> **AO1**
>
> Interact with others, shaping meanings through suggestions, comments and questions and drawing ideas together.

This means that you will need to work with others and pull ideas together through discussion.

> **AO1**
>
> Create and sustain different roles.

This means that you will need to take part in different role-play situations. Your principal task is to stay in character.

Speaking, Listening and Spoken Language

Section B
AO2 Spoken Language

AO2

Understand variations in spoken language, exploring why language changes in relation to contexts.

This means that you need to show that you understand how speech is used in different ways in different contexts.

AO2

Evaluate the impact of spoken language choices in your own and others' use.

This means that you need to think about the effects created by your own language choices and those of others.

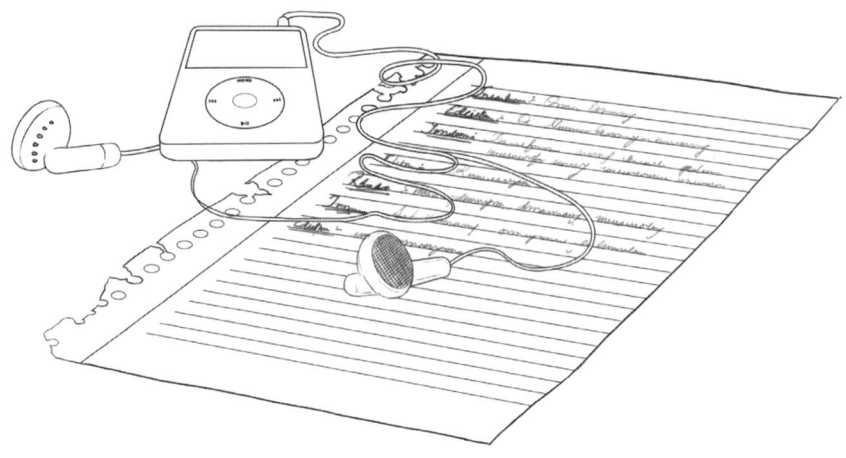

Speaking, Listening and Spoken Language

Section A: Speaking and Listening

Communicating and adapting language

Your speaking and listening assessment will require you to use language in different ways according to the particular context, purpose and audience of your speech. You will be assessed in **three** contexts:
- an individual activity involving presenting to an audience
- participating in a group discussion
- a drama-focused activity

One of the tasks must be based on a real-life situation. In all three contexts you will need to adapt your use of language to suit your audience and purpose.

Giving an individual presentation

When giving your individual presentation you will need to:
- make sure you express yourself clearly so that your audience can understand what you are saying
- use Standard English and avoid colloquial or slang expressions unless you are using them to create a particular effect
- make sure your presentation is effectively structured and you can sustain it – don't run out of things to say after the first minute
- be prepared to answer questions and listen to the views of others – if you don't know the answer to a question, say so.

Speaking, Listening and Spoken Language

Planning your talk
1. Begin by writing down all your ideas on the topic of your presentation.
2. Decide on your key points and structure your ideas. Plan your points in note form – don't write them out as an essay.
3. Writing down prompts can be useful but don't write down more than a few words for each point. You should **not** read from notes when giving your talk.

Choose one or more of the example tasks below and plan out a presentation. Try presenting it to a group of other students in your class.

Example tasks
1. Talk to your group about your favourite kind of music saying what appeals to you about it, what it means to you and why.
2. A group of students from another local school is visiting your class. Give a talk to them about your school giving the most positive impression you can.
3. Give a talk to a group of your peers about your work experience. This can either be work experience organized by your school or a particular holiday job that you have.
4. 'Things were different in my day.' Talk to your group about your views about how society has changed since you were a child.

Interacting and responding

This part of your assessment will usually take place in the form of a discussion as part of a group.

In order to do well you will need to:
- ensure that your contributions to the discussion are thoughtful and relevant
- interact and respond to others, which means listening carefully to what others have to say, exchanging comments or ideas and responding to them
- be prepared to challenge the views and ideas put forward by others but do so in a polite way, e.g. don't try to talk over them or shout them down

Speaking, Listening and Spoken Language

- develop your ideas by asking questions and making comments. Thoughtful questions and comments are central to effective discussion.

Example tasks
The tasks you undertake here could be either functional or literary based. Look at the examples below.
1. In a group of three or four discuss a topic which has recently been in the news.
2. In a group of three or four discuss your views and ideas on a set text you have all studied.
3. Discuss the problems caused by anti-social behaviour and what can be done to prevent it.
4. Discuss a filmed version of a play you have all seen.

Choose one of the tasks from the list above and, with a partner or small group, try a practice discussion. Ask someone else to listen and then give feedback on how each person spoke and behaved.

Summary of dos and don'ts

Do...	Don't...
listen carefully to what others say	interrupt while someone else is speaking
make relevant comments and contributions	try to talk over other people
give reasons to support your views	dominate the discussion
show that you appreciate the views of others even if you don't agree with them	listen without contributing
	dismiss the views of others
speak clearly and use straightforward language that everyone can understand	mumble or speak so quietly that others cannot hear you

Speaking, Listening and Spoken Language

Chairing a group discussion

You might be asked to chair a group discussion or be the group's leader. If you are the leader of a group discussion, you have to think about a few extra things too. For example:
- you will need to make sure that all members of the group get a chance to contribute
- if the discussion dries up, you will need to be ready to step in with a question or comment that will prompt further discussion
- you will need to make sure that conflicts don't break out – if an argument seems to be developing, step in to make sure that both sides have their say and listen to each other. This is very important – otherwise the discussion will break down.

Speaking, Listening and Spoken Language

Creating and sustaining roles

For this element of your Speaking and Listening assessment you will take part in a task which involves taking on a particular role. You will need to use various dramatic techniques and work on both scripted and improvised tasks.

Your role-play could take many forms. For example you might be asked to take part in a scenario involving:
- a real-life situation
- a situation based on a literary text you have studied
- a monologue
- a 'hot-seating' activity.

Example tasks

Look at the example tasks listed below.

1. You have arrived at a hotel where you are booked in for a week but the room is terrible and not at all as described on the Internet. You demand to see the manager. Enact the scene.
2. You were a witness of a serious fire. You are being interviewed by a journalist. Enact the scene.
3. Assume the role of a key character in a text you have studied and explain and justify your actions.
4. Take the role of a shop assistant dealing with a difficult customer.
5. Imagine you are a director making a film of a play you have studied. Choose a particular scene and give instructions to the actors about what you want them to do and how you want them to act the scene.

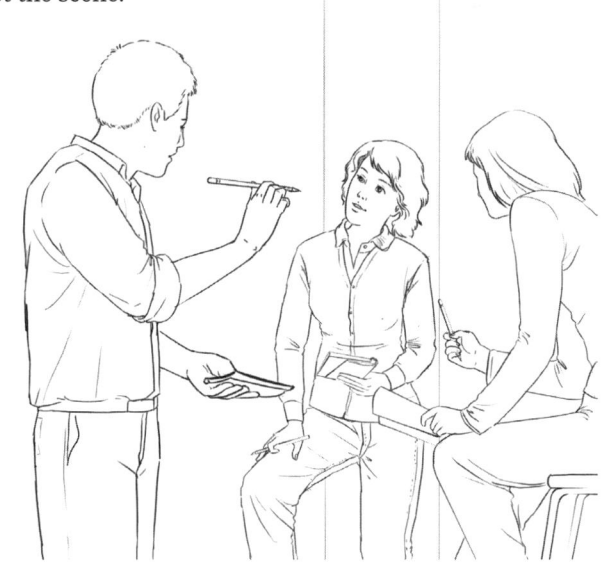

Speaking, Listening and Spoken Language

Try working on the following role-play with a partner.

Example role-play situation 1

Situation
A new housing development is being planned on the outskirts of your town. Currently the land is a partly wooded, wild area where people often go for walks.

A local radio station has sent an interviewer to find out the views of local people. The interviewer has asked you to give your views on the proposed development. Enact the interview.

Roles
A local resident
The interviewer from the radio station

Work on the following role-play with four other students.

Example role-play situation 2

Situation
You are a police officer who has been called to a supermarket car park. There has been a minor accident. A driver, reversing out of a parking space, has collided with another car reversing out of another space. No one has been injured but both cars have been damaged. The drivers are arguing about who is to blame as you arrive on the scene. Two people witnessed the accident. Enact what happens next.

Roles
A police officer
Driver 1
Driver 2
Witness 1
Witness 2

Speaking, Listening and Spoken Language

Section B: Spoken language

As you will know from your studies, spoken language differs in many ways from written language. One key difference is the significance of **non-verbal** features. When you write your response to this assessment task, you will have the opportunity to comment on how people **behave** when they speak as well as what they say. This includes aspects such as their pace, volume, use of pauses, tone of voice and body language.

Commenting on non-verbal features

Non-verbal features of speech can reveal a lot about the **relationships** between the participants. Practise analysing some of these features by reading the transcripts below and answering the questions that follow. In Transcript 1 an assistant teacher attempts to give instructions to a class of college students. In Transcript 2 a speaker begins a presentation to a group of local residents.

Transcript 1

Speaker A	Hi everyone... erm... I'd just like to...
Speaker B	(loudly) Ha ha, look at Steve!
Speaker A	I'd just like to...
Speaker C	(turning around, then loudly) Ahhhhh! You idiot! How did y-?
Speaker B	(loud) What are y'playing at?
Speaker A	(louder) Right! So... if... (faster) once everyone is settled I'd...
Speaker B	Ha ha! Where's y'bag?

Speaking, Listening and Spoken Language

Transcript 2

Speaker A   Good morning everyone and thank you for travelling here this morning. I know we have quite a lot to get through in this first session so I'll try to keep this brief.

Speaker B   (fast) Sorry I'm late (sits).

Speaker A   (nods) Our first speaker is Mr Jack Wilson.

Speaker C   Thanks Phil, right good morning everyone... is this working? I'm very bad with technology, especially before 9am (laughs).

Audience   (laughs)

Speaker C   Okay, right we are, thanks Phil – so, my name is Jack Wilson and I'm here on behalf of Think Advantage.

Answer the following questions relating to these transcripts.

1. What do Speaker A's pauses suggest in Transcript 1?
2. Which speaker appears to be dominating the situation in Transcript 1 and how can you tell? Think about:
   - pace (how fast)
   - volume (how loud)
   - body-language (movement)
   - turn-taking (how people take turns to speak).
3. Why does Speaker A change the volume and pace of his/her speech later in the Transcript 1?
4. What does the use of laughter signify in Transcript 1?
5. How does Speaker B show respect for the other speakers in Transcript 2?
6. Why does Speaker A nod in Transcript 2 and what might it reveal about his or her attitude to Speaker B?
7. What does Speaker C's laughter tell you in Transcript 2 and what are the effects of this?

Speaking, Listening and Spoken Language

Levels of formality

People speak in different ways according to how formal the situation is.

In the case of the speech that you will study for your assessment, you will already know where and why it took place so you should have some sense of what to expect. Some speeches, however, may not always go as planned.

Look at the grid below and decide which features might suggest a formal situation and which might suggest a less formal situation.

Feature	Formal	Informal
lots of laughter		
use of colloquial or dialect words		
lots of short exclamations		
use of Standard English		
shouting		
polite terms of address, e.g. 'Mr', 'Good morning'		
rhetorical devices		
unfinished utterances		
use of first names and nicknames		

Different kinds of speech

Like writing, all speech acts have a **purpose**, address a particular **audience** and are set within a particular **context**. These factors will have a major influence on the form that the speech takes, the kind of language used and the level of formality.

When chatting with a friend, for example, you would probably use a different kind of speech to that you would use if you were being interviewed for a job. It is likely that the first would be informal and the second very formal.

Speaking, Listening and Spoken Language

Spontaneous speech

Spontaneous speech is speech which is not planned-out beforehand. It is sometimes called **unplanned speech**. The vast majority of the speech that we use on a day-to-day basis is of this kind.

The majority of spontaneous speech consists of ungrammatical units called **utterances**. These reflect the fact that people do not have to speak in complete, grammatically correct sentences to be understood.

Here are some features to look out for in spontaneous speech:
- **turn-taking** – most conversation between two or more participants involves taking turns to speak (although not always in a regular pattern)
- **adjacency pairs** – we use these all the time in conversation: adjacency pairs are where one utterance leads to another – one speaker says something and another speaker says something in response, e.g. speaker A asks a question and speaker B answers
- **pauses** – these happen a lot in spontaneous speech; they can be used for emphasis or can signify that a speaker is considering what to say next
- **voice-filled pauses** – these are gaps in the conversation that are filled by some kind of non-verbal sound e.g. 'erm', 'er', 'um', etc.
- **fillers** – these fill gaps in the conversation but they are words rather than sounds, e.g. 'you know', 'I mean', 'well', etc.
- **overlaps** – these occur where one speaker begins speaking before another speaker has finished, or where both speak at the same time
- **repetitions** – these often occur when a speaker is searching for the right word or perhaps if he or she wishes to stress a particular point
- **false starts** – these sometimes happen when a speaker begins to speak and then corrects himself or herself by beginning the utterance again
- **end clipping** – this is when letters are dropped from the ends of words, e.g. 'happenin'' instead of 'happening'
- **contractions** – this is when words are shortened by running them together, e.g. 'don't' instead of 'do not'
- **slang or colloquial language** – this is frequently used in informal spontaneous speech.

Speaking, Listening and Spoken Language

When spontaneous speech is represented in the form of a **transcript**, it will be presented in such a way as to give an indication of how it was originally spoken.

Sometimes abbreviations are used in transcripts to indicate features, such as those listed below.

Key

(.)	micropause
(0.5)	pause of 0.5 seconds
underlining	emphasis of particular word
[	overlap

Look at the short extract from a transcript below. It records a discussion between two Year 10 students speaking about a film they saw recently.

Transcript

Speaker A	well (.) I thought it were crap
Speaker B	I really (erm) liked (.) it were good…
Speaker A	yeah (.) I might a known (.) you'd like (.) soppy stuff like that (.) it were crap (.) dont know how I managed to sit through it (.) I'm sayin (.)
Speaker C	well I thought it was good and I…
	[
Speaker A	gi it a rest (.) I don't even wanna think about it…

Look at the transcript above and identify features of spontaneous speech. Give an example of each.

When analysing spontaneous speech, as well as identifying features you should also explain what they reveal about the speakers and their attitudes to one another.

Speaking, Listening and Spoken Language

Boost your grade

Section A: Speaking and listening

The points below suggest ways of achieving the best grade in your speaking and listening assessments.

Communicating and adapting language
- Be confident when putting across information, ideas and feelings, emphasising significant points.
- Adapt and shape your talk effectively to suit the particular context, audience and purpose.
- Use well-chosen Standard English vocabulary and grammar appropriate to the situation.

Interacting and responding
- Listen carefully to what is said and respond to it in a thoughtful and considered way by asking questions.
- Respond to others ideas to develop points in a positive way.
- Initiate and develop discussion through purposeful continioutions.

Creating and sustaining roles
- Create convincing and complex characters and roles through appropriate dramatic techniques.
- Respond dynamically and sensitively in role, and explore ideas and issues while remaining in character.

Speaking, Listening and Spoken Language

Section B: Spoken language

The points below suggest ways of boosting your grade in your study of spoken language.
- show perception and originality in your answer
- show an analytical understanding of language variation and how you and others choose and adapt features of spoken language to create effects.
- support your answers with well-chosen references to texts or data
- show how spoken language is influence by context.

Unit 3
Information and Ideas

Exam insight

Unit summary

This unit is worth 40% of the overall GCSE English Language mark. It is divided into two sections.

Unit 3: Information and Ideas

Section A: Non-fiction and Media (20%)

Section B: Writing Information and Ideas (20%)

Section A: Non-fiction and media

This part of the unit tests your **reading skills**. You will be given a selection of materials to read in the exam and you will be required to answer several questions based on them.

Section B: Writing information and ideas

This part of the unit tests your **writing skills**. You will be asked to produce **one** piece of wrting on a topic broadly linked to the reading material you were given in Section A.

Assessment Objectives

This unit tests Assessment Objectives 3 and 4. Here is a breakdown of the skills tested.

Section A

AO3 Reading

AO3

Read and understand texts, selecting material appropriate to purpose, collating from different sources and making comparisons and cross-references as appropriate.

Information and Ideas

This means that you will need to understand the texts you read and choose appropriate material from them to answer questions. It also means that you will need to compare material from texts and make cross-references.

AO3
Develop and sustain interpretations of writers' ideas and perspectives.

This means that you will need to interpret ideas expressed by writers and show that you understand their views. You will need to comment on inferences and discuss how writers make their meaning clear.

AO3
Explain and evaluate how writers use linguistic, grammatical, structural and presentational features to achieve effects and engage and influence the reader.

This means you need to explain clearly how writers use language and (if relevant) use features such as headlines and illustrations to create effects and influence the reader.

Section B
AO4 Writing

AO4
Write to communicate clearly, effectively and imaginatively, using and adapting forms and selecting vocabulary appropriate to task and purpose in ways which engage the reader.

This means that you should write effectively using language to suit the particular audience and purpose of the task you have been given.

AO4
Organize information and ideas into structured and sequenced sentences, paragraphs and whole texts, using a variety of linguistic and structural features to support cohesion and overall coherence.

Information and Ideas

This means that you should organize your ideas into sentences and paragraphs that link together to create an effective piece of writing.

> **AO4**
> Use a range of sentence structures for clarity, purpose and effect, with accurate punctuation and spelling.

This means that you should use different kinds of sentences to suit the purpose of your writing. You should also ensure that your spelling and punctuation are accurate.

Section A: Reading non-fiction and media texts

In this section of the unit you will be looking at how writers express their ideas and the importance of presentation, style and language choice in their work. You will analyse what you read to interpret the writer's meaning, bearing in mind that your own experiences and attitudes may affect this interpretation.

When you sit the exam, it is essential that you read the questions carefully and are absolutely clear about what they are asking you to do.

Analysing your texts

Before you start to answer any questions it is suggested that you read the texts through at least **twice**. The points below outline things you can do to improve your understanding of the texts.

- Be aware of the kind of text you are reading. The information given on the exam paper may give you a clue, for example:

> ▸ *Destruction in the City*
> By referring to the presentation of the article and the language used by the eyewitnesses, explore how the website conveys to the reader the horror of the experience.

title gives a clue about the topic

tells you it is a website

UNIT 3: INFORMATION AND IDEAS

Information and Ideas

- Think about the **context** of the piece of writing – how does it influence the way the material is presented?
- Look at the way the **language** is used – annotating the text by underlining or highlighting key phrases can be useful.
- Look at other **presentational features** such as headlines, captions, pictures and the general layout. Think about the **effects** these features create.
- Note the writer's **style** – look for patterns such as the use of repetition or the use of particular imagery.

Close reading involves looking not only at the **meaning** of the text but also at **how** that meaning is created and conveyed to the reader.

Find an example for yourself of a non-fiction text of one or two pages in length. Read it carefully at least twice and then write down your ideas on the topics shown here. You could use a grid like the one below to record your thoughts.

Context	What is the context of the text?
Language	How is language used in different ways? Pick out some examples and explain/analyse the effects created.
Presentational features	Are features such as headlines, captions, pictures and illustrations used? If so, explain the effects they create. What about the layout? Does it contribute to the overall effect of the text?
Style	What kind of style does the writer use? Comment on two or three specific examples.

Commenting on language choices

Language choice is always closely linked to content as well as audience and purpose.

The plan below suggests one possible approach to writing about language.

Stage 1 – Content
Read the whole text to get a general idea of what it is about. Re-read the text annotating or highlighting key words and phrases that stand out.

Information and Ideas

Stage 2 – Audience and purpose

Think about the audience and purpose of the text:
- **who** it is aimed at (the audience)
- **why** it was written (the purpose).

Stage 3 – Effects

Look at how language is used to **appeal** to the audience and achieve the purpose.

Remember
- use examples of words and short phrases to support and illustrate your points
- comment on the **specific effects** created by the examples of language you have selected.

Use the **point – evidence – comment** approach.

Make sure your examples are:
- well-chosen and appropriate
- short and concise
- supporting the points you wish to make.

Select a text of your own and try using the approach above to write an analysis of how language is used to help the text to achieve its purpose.

Information and Ideas

Section B: Writing information and ideas

In this section of the unit you will be concentrating on the production of **one** piece of writing in the exam. It could be writing that performs a specific function or accomplishes a specific task. This is known as **functional** or **transactional** writing and includes letters, advertisements, information sheets, advice leaflets and emails. Or it could be a piece of **discursive** writing which involves discussing a topic and presenting your ideas about it.

Transactional writing

When practising a piece of transactional writing you need to be clear in your mind about four key things.
1. The **purpose** of the piece of writing – **why** you are writing it: what is it intended to achieve?
2. The **audience** of this piece of writing – **who** is it aimed at?
3. The **format** – what form will your writing take?
4. The **context** of the piece of writing: under what circumstances is the piece of writing being written?

The purpose, audience, format and context of the writing you will produce in the exam will be specified in the question.

Purpose
Before you write anything, it's vital that you know **why** you are writing. The exam question will provide this information for you so make sure you read it carefully.

> Each of the tasks below ask you to write for a different purpose. What is the main purpose of each one?
> - a letter of application for a job
> - a film review
> - a campaign leaflet about reducing pollution.

The purpose of what you write will affect **how** you write, which means the language you use, the way you structure your text and the tone you take. Try to make your writing as authentic as possible. You may have read similar texts yourself. What features

Information and Ideas

did they have? You will gain good marks if you can incorporate these elements into your own writing.

Use the table below to match each text to its main purpose.

Text	Main purpose
1. a letter of complaint about a faulty product	A. to encourage people to visit soon to buy something
2. a newspaper article about a recent archaeological discovery	B. to inform people about good and bad points, before giving an overall verdict
3. a review of a skate park	C. to persuade people to make a donation or support a cause
4. a campaign leaflet for a local charity	D. to provide interesting facts and information
5. a leaflet about the risks of driving carelessly	E. to demonstrate that you are unhappy about something and that you want something to be done about it
6. an advertisement for a new designer shop	F. to shock people and make them aware of the dangers involved; to persuade them to act more responsibly

For each text listed, identify one way that the main purpose will influence how you write. The first two have been done for you:

1. *I will need to make it clear exactly what is wrong with the product.*
2. *I will need to say when and where the discovery was made.*

Information and Ideas

Audience

The style of your writing will also be heavily affected by **who** the piece of writing is for. You would write an email to your local councillor, for example, in a different way to an email to your best friend. The checklist below shows features that are likely to be affected by the audience.

1. **Form of address** – how will you address your readers? For example: Dear Sir; Ladies and gentlemen; Hi mate; Attention all shoppers!
2. **Choice of vocabulary** – colloquial, technical, concise or emotive?
3. **Sentence structure** – short simple sentences, long complex sentences or a variety?
4. **Layout** – use of subheadings, bullet-point lists, tables, headlines, fact boxes?
5. **Choice of pronoun** – first-person (I), second-person (you) or third-person (he/she/they)?
6. **Tone** – humorous, objective, friendly, emotive, energetic or angry?

Format

When producing a piece of transactional writing you need to be clear about its **format** (or form), and adapt your **style** accordingly. For example, a letter requires a different layout and style of writing from an advertisement.

An application has been made to the planning department of your local council to build a wind farm on the hill-side close to where you live. You wish to inform the council of your point of view.

Write a letter either supporting or objecting to the development.

Information and Ideas

Here is the opening of a student's response to this question:

> 7 High Street
> Brigtown
> Hartchester
> HC3 1XX
>
> 15.03.10
>
> Planning Department,
> Harchester County Council
> HC1 7YO
>
> Dear Mr Ramsden,
>
> I am writing to you concerning the proposed development of a wind farm on the hillside overlooking Skipwith Low Village. Although I am basically in favour of the development of renewable energy sources where appropriate I would like to register my objection to this particular development.
>
> There are several reasons why I do not think that this development is a good idea. Firstly, it is clear that the wind farm would be structured quite close to the village. This means that...

How do you think this student has adapted his/her style to suit the form of writing?

Here are some points you might have noted:
- letter layout
- formal opening to the letter
- clear statement of purpose
- formal style to suit the formal nature of task.

Information and Ideas

Thinking about the tasks

Before you actually begin your transactional writing task make sure that you read the whole task and take in the information it provides. Set aside time to think about:
- the purpose of your piece of writing
- the audience for your piece of writing
- the format of your writing
- the context of the piece of writing
- the style you will use
- the point of view you will convey.

The grid below includes some possible tasks. You are also given the format the writing should take. For each task think about the kind of style (language and any presentational features) that you would use. The first one has been completed to give you some ideas.

Task	Format	Style
a letter of application for a job	letter	Formal use of language. Key information given in clear and concise style. Written in continuous prose.
a feature for the school magazine describing a trip you have been on	article	
an information sheet for parents explaining the arrangements and equipment required for a school snowboarding trip	information sheet	
an advertisement to recruit new members for your band	advertisement	
a review of a television programme you have seen	review	
a report for your local newspaper about facilities for young people in your area	newspaper report/article	

Information and Ideas

Discursive writing

This kind of writing involves discussing a topic and presenting your ideas or arguments about it. Sometimes discursive writing can be functional too and in fact there is a great deal of overlap between discursive writing and transactional writing.

There are three basic approaches to writing a discursive piece of writing. You could:
- argue in favour of a particular view
- argue against a particular view
- discuss arguments for and against a topic in a more balanced way.

Discursive writing can exist in many formats and can focus on almost any topic. The language itself can be formal or informal and can be structured in many different ways. It is likely that the wording of the task itself will set the topic, format, audience and purpose for you and may even give you some context too.

Planning your response

When producing a piece of discursive writing your main aim is to present and develop your ideas and views as clearly and effectively as possible. The first thing you need to do is to establish what your view is on the given topic and what viewpoint you are going to take.

The steps below set out one approach to planning your response.
1. Think about the topic that you have been given and decide what your standpoint is in relation to it.
2. Think about arguments for and against your given topic.
3. Decide on the points that you want to make and the order in which you will approach them in your writing.
4. Decide on the evidence that you will use to illustrate and support your views.
5. Decide on how you are going to open your piece of writing.
6. Think about how you aim to conclude your piece of writing.

Remember – careful planning is the secret to creating an effective piece of discursive writing.

Information and Ideas

Developing your ideas

The **opening paragraph** of your piece of discursive writing is important because you need to use this to capture the interest of your reader and also to establish your viewpoint on the issue you wish to discuss.

In the **main body of the piece** of writing you need to develop your ideas in more detail. There are two different ways to tackle this.
1. Present your points from one viewpoint but make references to alternative views where appropriate, throughout your response.
2. Begin by stating a view that doesn't agree with the view you hold, giving reasons why some people hold this view. Go on to then counter this view by putting forward the arguments that support the view you hold.

Avoid simply listing all the points in favour of one view and then all the points in favour of the opposite view before ending with a 'what I think' paragraph.

The **concluding paragraph** is as important as the opening paragraph. It is where you sum-up your points and end with a final point that leaves your reader either convinced that your view is the right one or at least with something to think about.

Information and Ideas

Adapting style to format

When writing discursively you need to write in an appropriate style and format to suit the task you have been set. This involves using **discursive language**.

The list below provides some useful words and phrases that you can use when discussing views or presenting an argument.
- It is certainly true that...
- However...
- I believe that...
- In contrast to...
- Some people believe that...
- Perhaps the most important point is...
- Above all we must consider...
- Alternatively...
- Nevertheless...
- On the other hand...
- Similarly...
- This suggests that...

Using key words and phrases like those listed above can help you to shape your response and present your views to the reader in a persuasive way.

The techniques below can add further impact to your writing.

Rhetorical questions
These are questions that are used to make a point rather than acquire an answer. For example: *Is this the kind of government we want leading our country? Is this what we really want?*

Use of opposing views
You can present views and ideas that are opposite to the ones you hold yourself, then systematically countering these with your own points. This can make your own argument more convincing.

Using personal experiences
You can use personal experiences as evidence to support your points. This adds weight to your argument.

Information and Ideas

Look carefully at the following question.

Write an article for your local newspaper giving your views on the proposal to install Close Circuit Television throughout your village or town.

Follow the steps below to complete a response to the task.
1. List ideas both for and against the proposal.
2. Decide what your own view is on the issue.
3. Underline or put a star next to the points that you are going to use in your response.
4. Outline the structure for your article.
5. Write your opening paragraph.
6. Write the main body of your article using your plan. Remember to support your points with evidence where you can.
7. Write your concluding section. This needs to wrap-up your response effectively and leave the reader with something to think about.

Boost your grade

The key to success in Unit 3 is to have a clear understanding of the texts that you are given in Section A and the nature of the tasks set in Section B.

This means having a clear understanding of:
The **purpose** of the task and the **audience** it is aimed at. You also need a clear understanding of the **context** of the piece of writing and the **format** that the writing takes.

These details will be included in the question on the exam paper. The secret is to apply this information to the style of language you adopt to make your writing do the job you want it to.

Information and Ideas

To extend your knowledge of how language is used in different contexts you should look at 'real life' examples of different kinds of transactional and discursive writing.

Here is a checklist of the kinds of texts that you could look at:
- magazine articles
- advertisements
- guide books
- letters (formal and informal)
- reviews (books, films, DVDs, computer games etc.)
- newspaper reports
- comment pieces
- charity appeals
- online forums

Section A

You must:
- be able to select and organize your material effectively
- show a detailed understanding of the texts and express your ideas clearly and concisely
- be able to explain and evaluate how the writers use language and presentational features to achieve their effects and influence the reader.

Section B

You must:
- make sure that your writing is addressing your intended audience throughout
- write using an appropriate format for the task
- make sure the content of your writing is focussed on the task, contains the right level of detail and is always relevant
- structure your writing effectively
- use a style that suits your audience
- use a wide range of appropriate vocabulary to achieve your effects
- use accurate punctuation to make your meaning clear
- use accurate spelling
- make sure your use of tenses is consistent and correct.

Glossary

Glossary

Accent: a distinctive manner of pronunciation that marks a regional or social identity.

Adjacency pairs: in spoken language, a sequence of utterances that form a recognizable structure. Adjacency pairs follow each other, are produced by different speakers, have a logical connection, and conform to a pattern, e.g. questions and answers, commands and responses.

Adjective: a word that describes a noun – e.g. *the wooden table*; *the red balloon*. They can also indicate degree, e.g. *the tallest girl was the slowest*.

Adverb: a word that describes the action of a verb – e.g. *the boy ate hungrily*.

Alliteration: the repetition of the same consonant sound, especially at the beginning of words, e.g. 'five miles meandering with a mazy motion' (*Kubla Khan* by Samuel Taylor Coleridge).

Antithesis: contrasting ideas or words that are balanced against each other, e.g. 'To be, or not to be' (*Hamlet* by William Shakespeare).

Assonance: the repetition of similar vowel sounds, e.g. 'there must be Gods thrown down and trumpets blown' ('Hyperion' by John Keats). This features the paired assonance of *must, trum-* and *thrown, blown*.

Chaining: the linking together of adjacency pairs to form a conversation.

Colloquial: slang or non-standard features in speech or writing.

Conjunction: a word that connects other words, e.g. *and, but*.

Contraction: a shortened word, e.g. *isn't, don't*.

Dialect: a language variety marked by a distinctive grammar and vocabulary, used by people with a common regional or social background.

Dialogue: speech between two or more people.

Direct speech: the actual words spoken by a person, recorded in

Glossary

written form using speech marks or quotation marks.

Feedback: the reaction speakers receive from their listeners.

Formality: a scale of language use relating to the formality of the social context within which it is used. Language can be used formally or informally depending on the context.

Hyperbole: a deliberate and extravagant exaggeration.

Imagery: the use of words to create a picture or 'image' in the mind of the reader. Images can relate to any of the senses – not just sight, but also hearing, taste, touch and smell. The term is often used when referring to descriptive language, in particular the use of **metaphors** and **similes.**

Indirect speech: the words of a speaker that are reported rather than quoted directly – e.g. *David said that he was going out.* Direct speech would be: *"I am going out," said David.*

Interrogative: a question.

Intonation: the tone of voice in speech.

Metaphor: comparing one thing to another in order to make a description more vivid. Unlike a **simile**, a metaphor states that one thing *is* the other. For example, a simile could be *The wind cut through me like a knife*, whereas a metaphor might state *The wind cut through me.*

Narrative: a piece of writing or speech that tells a story.

Non-standard English: any variety of language use that does not conform to the standard, prestige form of English accepted as the norm by society.

Onomatopoeia: the use of words whose sounds copy the sounds of the thing they describe. On a simple level, words like *bang, hiss* and *splash* are onomatopoeic.

Purpose: the reason why a piece of writing has been written or a speech made – e.g. to entertain, to explain, to persuade or to argue.

Received pronunciation: sometimes known as RP, the prestige British accent that has a high social status and is not related to a specific region or influenced by regional variation.

Simile: comparing one thing to another in order to make a

Glossary

description more vivid. Similes use the words *like* or *as* to make the comparison.

Slang: distinctive words and phrases associated with informal speech. Very often it is used within certain social groups or age groups.

Standard English: the form of English considered to be and accepted as the norm in society, as used in government, education, law, etc. Language that differs form this standard is known as 'non-standard'.

Structure: the way that a poem, play or other piece of writing has been put together. This can include the metre pattern, stanza arrangement, the ways the ideas are developed, etc.

Synonym: a word with the same or nearly the same meaning as another word – e.g. *shut* and *close* or *ship* and *vessel*.

Tag question: a question added to the end of a sentence which requires a reply – e.g. *Terrible weather, isn't it?*

Tone: the tone of a text is created through the combined effects of a number of features, such as vocabulary, syntax and rhythm. The tone can be a major factor in establishing the overall impression of a piece of writing.

Transcript: a written record of spoken language, which may use symbols to represent non-verbal features of speech.

Turn-taking: organization of speakers' contributions in a conversation. Turns may be fairly equal, or one of the participants may dominate the dialogue.

Vocabulary: the words of a language.